# AMERICAN HISTORY ADDS UP

BY MARC GAVE

## Table of Contents

1. New Lands to Explore . . . . . . . . . . . . . . . . . . . . . 2

2. A New Nation . . . . . . . . . . . . . . . . . . . . . . . . . . 6

3. The Nation Divided . . . . . . . . . . . . . . . . . . . . . 14

4. New Frontiers, New Citizens. . . . . . . . . . . . . . . 18

5. Power Struggles . . . . . . . . . . . . . . . . . . . . . . . 23

6. A Final Frontier . . . . . . . . . . . . . . . . . . . . . . . 26

7. Gaining a Perspective: A Time Line
   of American History. . . . . . . . . . . . . . . . . . . . . 28

Solve This! Answers. . . . . . . . . . . . . . . . . . . . . . 30

Glossary . . . . . . . . . . . . . . . . . . . . . . . . . . . . . 31

Index . . . . . . . . . . . . . . . . . . . . . . . . . . . . . . . 32

# New Lands to Explore

In 1492, Italian explorer Christopher Columbus set out across the Atlantic Ocean. In just over two months, his ships—the *Niña*, the *Pinta*, and the *Santa María*—landed on San Salvador, an island in the Bahamas.

In the century after Columbus, many explorers visited what is now the United States. These explorers owed Columbus their success. Columbus dared to cross the ocean—and survived!

*Pacific Ocean*

↑ This map shows the routes of some of the explorers who came what is now the Uni States in the centu after Columbus.

←Christopher Colum

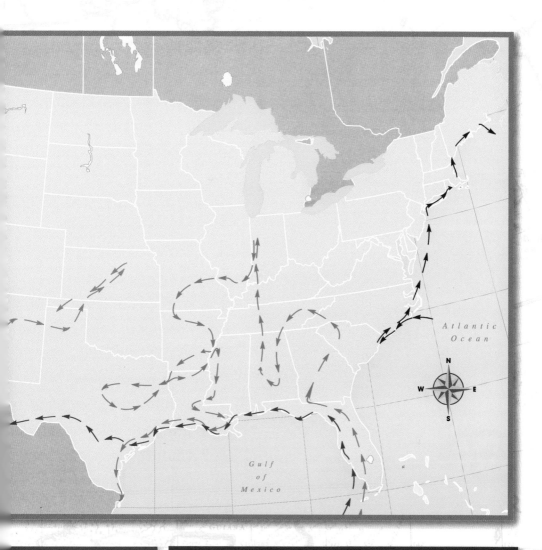

Atlantic
Ocean

N
W     E
S

Gulf
of
Mexico

# A TIMELINE OF EXPLORERS

Create a time line of the explorations on the map,
plus Columbus's first voyage. Start with 1490 and
plot lines for every 10 years until 1590. Then place
dots on the time line for the year each explorer
came to America. When a year falls between two
lines, estimate to decide where the dot goes.

3

← The Mayflower

Within one hundred years of the exploration of America, the Pilgrims arrived in the New World. They left England on September 16, 1620, crossed the Atlantic Ocean, and landed in Massachusetts on November 2.

The Pilgrims accounted for only 37 of the *Mayflower*'s 102 passengers. The other passengers were crew members or people whom the owners of the *Mayflower* required the Pilgrims to take along.

One hundred and thirteen years after the Pilgrims landed on Plymouth Rock, the last of the original thirteen colonies was settled.

**IT'S A FACT!**

The first permanent European **settlement** in what is now the United States was not in one of the thirteen original colonies. It was the Spanish settlement of St. Augustine, Florida, established in 1565.

The Queen Elizabeth (QE2), a modern ocean liner, can travel at 37 miles per h

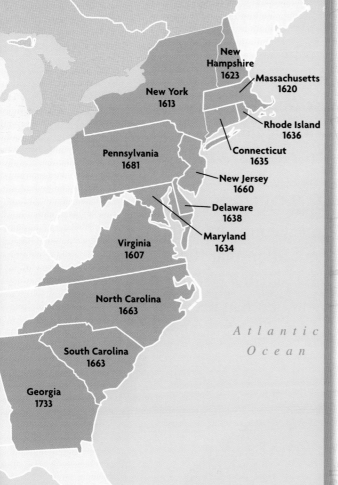

# THE ORIGINAL 13 COLONIES
## Dates of First Settlement

New Hampshire 1623

Massachusetts 1620

New York 1613

Rhode Island 1636

Connecticut 1635

Pennsylvania 1681

New Jersey 1660

Delaware 1638

Maryland 1634

Virginia 1607

North Carolina 1663

Atlantic Ocean

South Carolina 1663

Georgia 1733

## SOLVE THIS!

**1** How many days did it take the Mayflower to cross the Atlantic, counting the day the ship left and the day it arrived?

The distance between England and Massachusetts is about 3,200 miles. Use a calculator to figure out how many miles the Mayflower averaged per day.

About how long would it take the QE2 to cover the same distance?

**2** Make a table with the names of the thirteen original colonies in the left column and the dates of their first settlement in the right column. Order the colonies from earliest settlement to latest.

5

# A New Nation

On April 18, 1775, Paul Revere waited for a lantern signal from the Old North Church in Boston. "One if by land, and two if by sea," would tell how the British were coming. Soon Paul Revere would begin his famous midnight ride to let the **patriots** know that the British were going to attack.

Revere was captured by the British, but two other riders got through. When the British arrived at Concord the next morning to destroy guns and ammunition that the colonists were storing, the patriots were ready. The American Revolution had begun!

**IT'S A FACT!**

On horseback an on foot, it took a long time to get from place t place in colonial America. Maybe that's why the war lasted six an a half years—and battles continue to be fought lon after the British surrendered!

Paul Revere was also a famous silversmith.

It was from the Old North Church in Boston, Massachusetts, that Paul Revere began his famous ride.

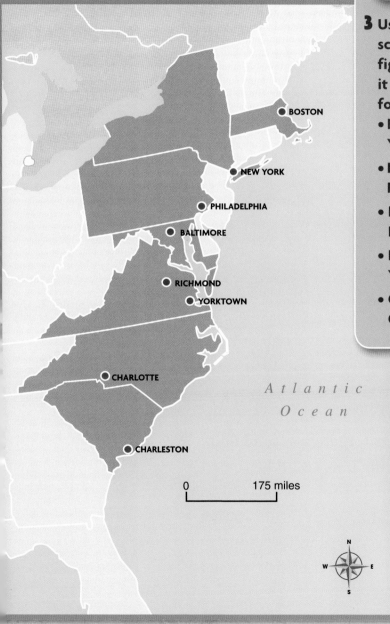

BOSTON

NEW YORK

PHILADELPHIA

BALTIMORE

RICHMOND

YORKTOWN

CHARLOTTE

CHARLESTON

Atlantic Ocean

0        175 miles

N
W    E
S

## SOLVE THIS!

**3** Use the mileage scale on the map to figure out how far it is between the following cities:

- Boston and New York
- New York and Philadelphia
- Philadelphia and Baltimore
- Richmond and Yorktown
- Charlotte and Charleston

←
money issued by the state of New Jersey

## THINK IT OVER!

Imagine that there was no standard money system and you could make up your own.
- What would you decide to use for money?
- What would you call your units (like a penny or a dollar) of money?

Because the British government had not allowed the colonists to make their own coins, they made paper money instead. By the mid 1700s, there was more paper money in the colonies than there was gold and silver for which the bills could be traded. So the British ordered the colonists to stop making paper money. As a result, during the Revolutionary War, and for a long time afterwards, colonists used British, French, and Spanish money.

## WHAT DOES IT COST?

Even after the U.S. government was formed, people could still use foreign coins. State banks issued their own notes, which sometimes proved to be worthless. And how much something cost often depended on what you were using to pay for it

Soon after the United States of America as formed, the first U.S. **census**—the ounting of the people in the country—took lace. Since that first one in 1790, there has en a census every ten years. Of course, nsuses aren't always exact—people are orn, move, and die while the census is ing taken.

Below is a chart with information from e 1790 census. The population of each ate is given in thousands.

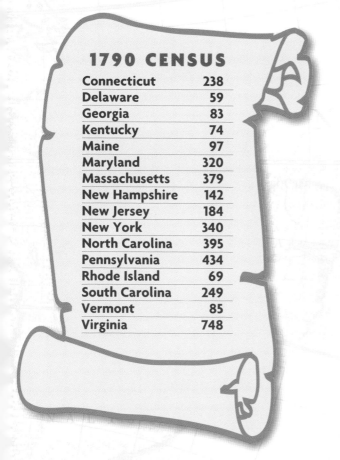

**1790 CENSUS**

| | |
|---|---|
| Connecticut | 238 |
| Delaware | 59 |
| Georgia | 83 |
| Kentucky | 74 |
| Maine | 97 |
| Maryland | 320 |
| Massachusetts | 379 |
| New Hampshire | 142 |
| New Jersey | 184 |
| New York | 340 |
| North Carolina | 395 |
| Pennsylvania | 434 |
| Rhode Island | 69 |
| South Carolina | 249 |
| Vermont | 85 |
| Virginia | 748 |

**SOLVE THIS!**

**4** Which three states had the largest populations in 1790?

Which three states had the smallest?

About 8 million people live in New York City today. Is that half as many, about the same, or twice as many people as were living in all of the states on the chart in 1790?

In 1803, the United States purchased a vast region of North American territory from France. This land, called the Louisiana Purchase, almost doubled the area of the United States, expanding the country westward. The Louisiana Purchase would later be divided into thirteen states—all of some states and just parts of others.

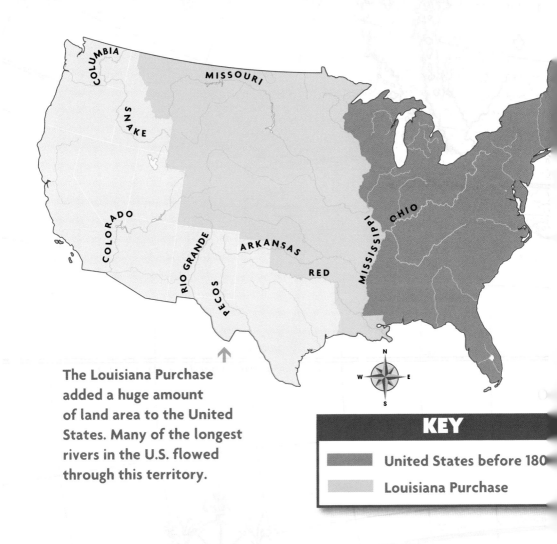

The Louisiana Purchase added a huge amount of land area to the United States. Many of the longest rivers in the U.S. flowed through this territory.

**KEY**

United States before 180

Louisiana Purchase

In 1804, President Thomas Jefferson hired
eriwether Lewis and William Clark to
:plore the Louisiana Territory. They often
llowed rivers in their journey westward.

## TEN LONGEST RIVERS IN THE U.S.

Rivers have always been important in American history. Here are the ten longest rivers in the United States today.

|  |  |
|---|---|
| Missouri | 2,540 miles |
| Mississippi | 2,340 miles |
| Yukon | 1,980 miles |
| St. Lawrence | 1,900 miles |
| Rio Grande | 1,900 miles |
| Arkansas | 1,460 miles |
| Colorado | 1,450 miles |
| Atchafayla | 1,420 miles |
| Ohio | 1,310 miles |
| Red | 1,290 miles |

## SOLVE THIS!

5 The farthest you can travel downriver in the United States is by taking the Red Rock to the Missouri to the Mississippi to the Gulf of Mexico. The Red Rock is 225 miles long. If the whole trip covers 3,710 miles, how far is it along the Mississippi from the mouth of the Missouri to the Gulf of Mexico?

In the late 1840s and early 1850s, many Easterners headed toward California. They had a choice of three equally difficult routes to get there. Along any route, the trip could take up to six months. One route was by ship around the tip of South America. Another was by ship to Panama, overland at its narrowest point, and then by ship again to California. The last was by foot or covered wagon through the wilderness and over the mountains of American territory.

What drew half a million people to California in those days? Gold fever! Most gold is found in rock deep within Earth. But in January 1848, gold was discovered in California's American River. Within a year, the gold rush was on.

Gold was later discovered in Colorado (1858), Nevada (along with silver, 1859), and Alaska (1896), among other places.

A poster from 1849 advertises passage to San Francisco, California, from New Bedford, Massachusetts.

## SOLVE THIS!

**6** The price of gold rises and falls. At the time this book was written, gold was valued at about $260 an ounce. If you were worth your weight in gold, how much would that be?

*Atlantic Ocean*

*Pacific Ocean*

N
W    E
S

**IT'S A FACT!**

The nickname for people who took part in the gold rush was Forty-Niners, which was the year that most of them left home.

...ericans who lived
...the East Coast
...ually traveled by
...a. Those who lived
...and usually took
...e land route. It
...s shorter, but
...t faster.

**KEY**

 overland

 by ship

by ship and overland

# The Nation Divided

Only a little more than ten years after the gold rush, a different kind of fever swept the country: war fever. Some people believe the Civil War was fought over slavery. Others believe it was fought over states' rights. Still others believe it was an economic war.

↑ **Abraham Lincol▶**

By the election of 1860, the country was deeply divided. Abraham Lincoln, the Republican Party nominee, took a moderately antislavery position and had little support in the South. The Democratic Party nominated Stephen Douglas, but southern delegates split off and nominated their own candidate, John C. Breckenridge. A fourth candidate, John Bell, was nominated by the Constitutional Union Party.

Lincoln did not win a majority of the popular votes. But he won the majority of votes in the **Electoral College**, which is necessary to become president.

**IT'S A FACT!**

By 1861, there were tw▶ American presidents. Jefferson Davis was chosen president of th▶ Confederate States of America after eleven southern states **seced**▶ withdrew—from the U▶

ephen Douglas

↑ John C. Breckenridge

↑ John Bell

**KEY**

- A. Lincoln
- J. Bell
- S. Douglas
- J. Breckenridge

**7** How many electoral votes did each candidate get in the election of 1860? What was the total number of electoral votes cast in the election?

If a candidate needed more than half of the total votes to win the White House, how many did Lincoln have to get?

← A cotton plantation in the South around 185- is depicted in this painting.

In many ways the North and the South were two countries even before the southern states seceded. Most of the manufacturing was in the North. The South's economy depende- on exporting cotton. A majorit of the wealthiest people lived i the South. And almost a third - free Southerners owned slaves.

## SLAVE POPULATIONS IN THE SOUTH

- 47 percent of the population in the lower South (Alabama, Florida, Georgia, Louisiana, Mississippi, South Carolina, Texas) were slaves.
- 29 percent of the population in the upper South (Arkansas, North Carolina, Tennessee, Virginia) were slaves.
- 13 percent of the population in the border states (Delaware, Kentucky, Maryland, Missouri) were slaves.

47% lower South

29% upper South

13% border states

ND
5

MN
2

ID
1

PA
2

IN
1

OH
2

D.C.
1

CO
1

WV
15

VA
123

MD
7

KS
4

MO
27

KY
11

NC
20

NM
2

OK
7

AR
17

TN
38

SC
11

*Atlantic Ocean*

MS
16

AL
7

GA
31

TX
5

LA
23

FL
6

*Gulf of Mexico*

**KEY**

territories where battles took place

states where battles took place

The 385 main battles of the Civil War (1861–1865) took place in 20 states, 5 **territories**, and in the District of Columbia. Of all these battles, 123 occurred in Virginia alone. The next highest number was in Tennessee, with 38. Colorado, Idaho, New Mexico, North Dakota, and Oklahoma were all territories during the Civil War, not states.

**SOLVE THIS!**

**8** Use a calculator to figure out what percentage of the battles took place in Virginia. Which five states had the greatest number of battles?

The Manchester Print Works Factory in Manchester, New Hampshire, was one of many busy textile factories in the North. This engraving was done around 1854.

# New Frontiers, New Citizens

Following the Civil War, there was increased movement westward. The **frontier** lured many Americans with the promise of cheap land, new jobs, and a better life.

But the promise of the frontier wasn't without its problems. Towns and cities seemed to spring up overnight. Buildings went up quickly and without much thought. Roads were poor, rail transportation was scarce, and water and sewage systems barely existed.

Sometimes, cities had to be rebuilt. A fire destroyed Chicago in 1871 and an earthquake and fire leveled San Francisco in 1906.

## HOW MANY PEOPLE LIVED IN CITIES?

Here are the populations of some midwestern and western cities. A dash means that the city did not exist in 1850.

| | 1850 | 1900 |
|---|---|---|
| Chicago, IL | 29,963 | 1,698,5 |
| Denver, CO | -- | 133,8 |
| Houston, TX | 2,396 | 44,6 |
| Kansas City, MO | -- | 163,7 |
| Omaha, NE | -- | 102,5 |
| Portland, OR | -- | 90,4 |
| San Francisco, CA | 34,776 | 342,7 |
| Seattle, WA | -- | 80,6 |

## ✚ ✖ ➖ ✚ SOLVE THIS!

**9** Which city that existed in 1850 had the largest increase in population by 1900? How many times greater was its population in 1900 than in 1850?

e San Francisco
rthquake and fire,
06

→

the Chicago fire, 1871

↑
This painting shows the lower basin of Mammoth Hot Springs in Yellowstone National Park during the 1870s.

These immigrants, on a ship in New York Harbor, are on their way to Elli Island and looking at New York for the first time.

## HOW BIG ARE THESE PARKS?

National parks vary in size. They are usually measured in acres.

| PARK | ACRES |
| --- | --- |
| Yellowstone (WY, MT, ID) | 2,219,79" |
| Yosemite (CA) | 761,236 |
| Petrified Forest (AZ) | 93,533 |
| Everglades (FL) | 1,507,85C |
| Wrangell-St. Elias (AK) | 8,363,618 |
| Denali (AK) | 4,741,80C |
| Glacier Bay (AK) | 3,322,79⁴ |
| Acadia (ME) | 46,998 |
| Mammoth Cave (KY) | 52,83C |
| Carlsbad Caverns (NM) | 46,76C |

As the frontier became increasingly populated, Congress began to set aside some of the land "as a public park or pleasuring ground for the benefit and enjoyment of the people." In 1872, Yellowstone National Park, located in parts of Wyoming, Idaho, and Montana, became the first park of its kind anywhere.

Those heading west included not only native-born Americans but **immigrants** (IH-mih-grunts) as well. The United States has always been a land of immigran From the earliest settlers who came from Asia thousands of years ago, to the first Europea seeking their fortune or freedo of worship, to the most recent immigrants fleeing war and famine, people have come to the United States.

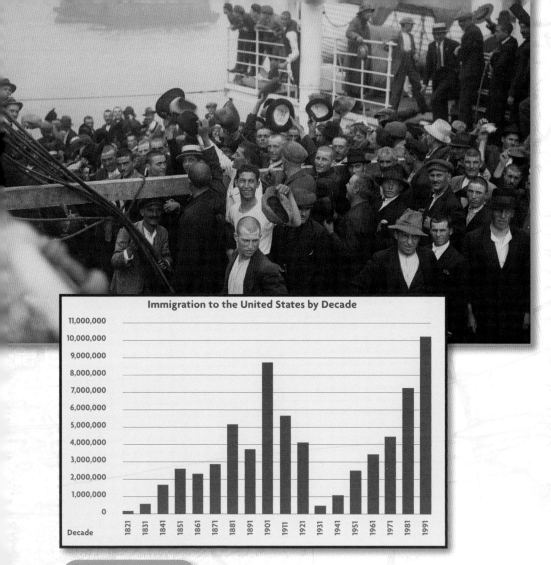

Immigration to the United States by Decade

Decade: 1821, 1831, 1841, 1851, 1861, 1871, 1881, 1891, 1901, 1911, 1921, 1931, 1941, 1951, 1961, 1971, 1981, 1991

⊕ ⊗ ⊖ ⊕

## SOLVE THIS!

**10** There are 640 acres in a square mile. Use this information and the chart on the opposite page to figure out:

- How many square miles are in Yellowstone Park.

- How many square miles are in Wrangell-St. Elias.

- How many of the parks in the list are larger than the state of Rhode Island, which is 1,565 square miles.

**11** During which decade has immigration been the highest? During which other decades has it also been high?

A family poses for a photograph on the porch of their ranch in California during the 1890s.

Life on the frontier was not easy. Those who settled there endured great hardship. In fact, life during this time might seem difficult to you! For example, can you imagine what life was like before electricity? When a new invention came along, it often took a long time before it was widely used.

## WHEN DID IT START RUNNING ON ELECTRICITY?

| | |
|---|---|
| Telephone | 1876 |
| Phonograph | 1877 |
| Light bulb | 1879 |
| Fan | 1882 |
| Iron | 1882 |
| Vacuum cleaner | 1907 |
| Radio receiver | 1913 |
| Toaster, automatic | 1918 |

# ower Struggles

While Europeans were streaming into the nited States, the most powerful ountries in Europe were on eir way to war. In the summer 1914, the **assassination** h-sa-sih-NAY-shun) of the eir (AIR) to the throne of ustria-Hungary set off World ar I. Before long, Austria-ungary and Germany (the entral Powers) were fighting reat Britain, France, and Russia he Allies). Other countries on joined in the fight.

The United States entered e war in 1917 and helped to n it in November 1918.

This poster from 1918 asks people to buy war bonds to help the United States pay for World War I.

**SOLVE THIS!**

**12** The total number of soldiers who fought in World War I was 65 million. Of those, 8.5 million died.
  • What percentage of the total number of soldiers died?
  • Of the 4.7 million American soldiers who fought, 117,000 died. Was that a smaller or larger percentage than worldwide?

# CHAPTER 5

Unemployed men wait in long lines for soup and bread during the Great Depression.

In October 1929, the **stock market** crashed. By 1933, stock was worth less than twenty percent of its top 1929 value. Businesses shut down, factories stopped operating, banks failed, and farm income fell fifty percent. About a quarter of the work force was out of a job. The Great Depression had begun.

## SOLVE THIS!

**13** On average, if something cost a dollar in 1933, it should cost about $13 today. So if a price now is more than 13 times the 1933 price, then the 1933 price was a bargain. Which of the foods listed were bargains in 1933?

## WAS IT A BARGAIN?

The left column shows prices from Indiana food stores in 1932–1933. The right column shows examples of today's prices. Prices where you shop may be different.

| | | |
|---|---|---|
| Bacon, sliced, 1 lb | $0.15 | $1.99 |
| Butter, 1 lb | 0.24 | 2.99 |
| Coffee, 1 lb | 0.32 | 2.99 |
| Hot dogs, 1 lb | 0.13 | 1.99 |
| Jell-O, 3 packages | 0.29 | 1.99 |
| Oranges, dozen | 0.29 | 2.99 |
| Peanut butter, 2 lb | 0.15 | 3.99 |
| Rice, 5 lb | 0.19 | 2.39 |
| Spaghetti, 3 lb | 0.25 | 1.49 |
| Strawberries, pint | 0.19 | 1.49 |

The United States did not lly recover from the Great epression until World War II, hen the economy focused on upporting the war effort.

As with World War I, the nited States did not enter World ar II when it started in 1939. It as not until December 7, 1941, hen the Japanese bombed Pearl arbor in Hawaii, that the United ates joined the fight.

**SOLVE THIS!**

**14** There are 2,000 pounds in a ton. What was the force of each atom bomb in pounds?

In August 1945, the United States dropped atom bombs on the Japanese cities of Hiroshima and Nagasaki. The attacks caused tremendous death and destruction and forced the Japanese to surrender.

The atom bomb that fell on Hiroshima had a force equal to 15,000 tons of TNT. The bomb that fell on Nagasaki had a force of 22,000 tons of TNT.

mushroom cloud forms om the atom bomb blast at roshima, August 6, 1945.

This is what Hiroshima looked like after the explosion of the atom bomb.

# CHAPTER 6

# A Final Frontier

In the 1950s, Americans turned their sights to a different frontier: space. As more and more space flights were planned, distances began to be measured in hundreds of thousands or hundreds of millions of miles.

On July 20, 1969, Neil Armstrong and Buzz Aldrin became the first astronauts to land on the moon. People throughout the nation and around the world shared the historic moment, watching as images of the moon's surface were transmitted by satellite to their television screens.

## SUCCESSFUL MOON LANDINGS

| | |
|---|---|
| Apollo 11 | July 20, 1969 |
| Apollo 12 | November 14, 1969 |
| Apollo 14 | January 31, 1971 |
| Apollo 15 | July 26, 1971 |
| Apollo 16 | April 16, 1972 |
| Apollo 17 | December 7, 1972 |

**Astronaut Buzz Aldrin stands beside an American flag placed on the moon during the Apollo 11 landing.**

Apollo 11 is seen on the launch pad atop the Saturn V rocket that launched it to the moon on July 16, 1969.

**SOLVE THIS!**

**15** If the moon is about 238,000 miles from Earth, about how many miles did U.S. astronauts travel round-trip on the six Apollo missions that resulted in successful moon landings?

Apollo 11 was the first of six successful issions that landed Americans on the moon. ere was also one near disaster. Apollo 13, ich left Earth on April 11, 1970, never ded on the moon because a serious ctrical problem developed. This problem ected the astronauts' life support system. rtunately, the astronauts were able to make ome home safely.

# CHAPTER 7

# Gaining a Perspective: A Time Line of American Histor

The United States, once part of a vast, unexplored continent, has a rich and complex history. Countless people and events have shaped our nation in the past, and will continue to do so in the future. This time line identifies some of the important moments in America's past: those of triumph and those of challenge.

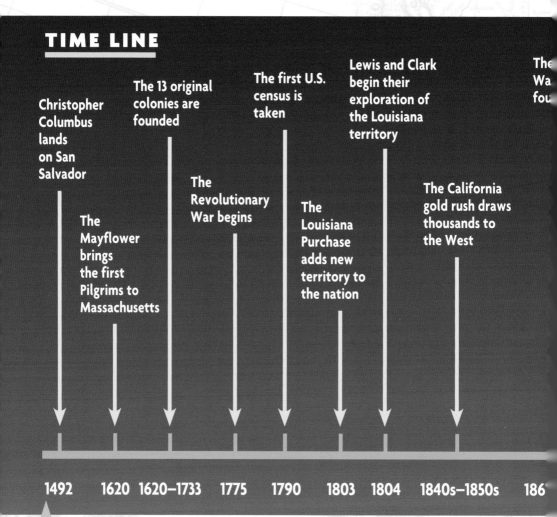

## TIME LINE

**Christopher Columbus lands on San Salvador**

**The Mayflower brings the first Pilgrims to Massachusetts**

**The 13 original colonies are founded**

**The Revolutionary War begins**

**The first U.S. census is taken**

**The Louisiana Purchase adds new territory to the nation**

**Lewis and Clark begin their exploration of the Louisiana territory**

**The California gold rush draws thousands to the West**

**The Wa fou**

| 1492 | 1620 | 1620–1733 | 1775 | 1790 | 1803 | 1804 | 1840s–1850s | 186 |

You have read about many important moments in America's history. Can you think of other events you would want to add to this time line? When did they occur? Why were they important?

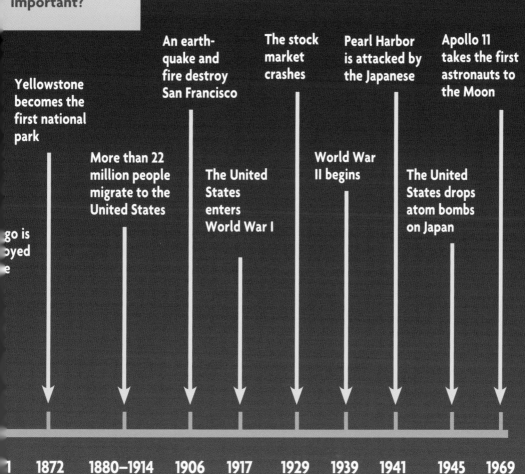

An earthquake and fire destroy San Francisco

The stock market crashes

Pearl Harbor is attacked by the Japanese

Apollo 11 takes the first astronauts to the Moon

Yellowstone becomes the first national park

More than 22 million people migrate to the United States

The United States enters World War I

World War II begins

The United States drops atom bombs on Japan

go is oyed e

| 1 | 1872 | 1880–1914 | 1906 | 1917 | 1929 | 1939 | 1941 | 1945 | 1969 |

# SOLVE THIS! ANSWERS

**1** Page 5
67 days; about 47.8 miles per day; 3.6 days

**2** Page 5
The order of settlement: Virginia, New York, Massachusetts, New Hampshire, Maryland, Connecticut, Rhode Island, Delaware, New Jersey, North Carolina, South Carolina, Pennsylvania, Georgia

**3** Page 7
Answers within 25 miles are reasonable: 160 miles; 90 miles; 77 miles; 57 miles; 155 miles

**4** Page 9
VA, PA, NC; DE, RI, KY; twice as many

**5** Page 11
1,170 miles

**6** Page 12
Answers will vary; the formula is weight in pounds x 16 (ounces) x $260 (dollars per ounce). At 80 pounds, for example, a student would be worth $332,800.

**7** Page 15
Lincoln, 180; Breckenridge, 72; Douglas, 12; Bell, 39; 303; 152

**8** Page 17
32 percent; VA, TN, GA, MO, and LA

**9** Page 18
Chicago; more than 56 times

**10** Page 21
3,468; 13,068; five: Yellowstone, Everglades, Wrangell-St. Elias, Denali, and Glacier Bay

**11** Page 21
1991–2000 (projected); 1901–10, 1981–90; 1911–20 are the next three highest.

**12** Page 23
13 percent; smaller (2 percent)

**13** Page 24
Bacon, hot dogs, and peanut butter

**14** Page 25
30 million pounds; 44 million pounds

**15** Page 27
About 2,856,000 miles (six round-trip journeys)

# Glossary

**assassination**     (uh-sa-sih-NAY-shun) planned killing, as of an important person (page 23)

**census**     (SEN-sus) a counting of people (page 9)

**Electoral College**     (ih-LEK-tuh-rul KAH-lij) a group of people called electors, chosen by state governments to actually vote for president of the United States (page 14)

**frontier**     (FRUN-teer) the edge of settlement (page 18)

**heir**     (AIR) a person who will inherit a title or money (page 23)

**immigrants**     (IH-mih-grunts) people from a foreign country who come to live in a new country (page 20)

**patriots**     (PAY-tree-uts) people who love and defend their country (page 6)

**seceded**     (sih-SEED-ed) left the United States (page 14)

**settlement**     (SEH-tul-ment) a new place where people make their homes, or the act of making a home in a new place (page 4)

**stock market**     (STAHK MAR-ket) a place where people buy and sell shares that companies offer to the public (page 24)

**territory**     (TAIR-ih-tor-ee) land; a land belonging to the United States but not yet a state (page 17)

# Index

Aldrin, Buzz, 26

American Revolution, 6

Armstrong, Neil, 26

assassination, 23

Bell, John, 14–15

Boston, 6–7

Breckenridge, John C., 14–15

British, 6, 8

California, 12

census, 9

Chicago fire, 18–19

Civil War, 14, 17–18

Columbus, Christopher, 2–3

Davis, Jefferson, 14

Douglas, Stephen, 14–15

election of 1860, 14–15

Electoral College, 14

England, 4

frontier, 18, 20, 26

gold rush, 12

Great Depression, 24

heir, 23

Hiroshima, Japan, 25

immigrant, 20

immigration, 20–21

Lewis and Clark, 11

Lincoln, Abraham, 14–15

Louisiana Purchase, 10

Louisiana Territory, 11

*Mayflower*, 4–5

moon, 26–27

Nagasaki, 25

national parks, 20–21

patriot, 6

Pearl Harbor, Hawaii, 25

Pilgrims, 4

Plymouth Rock, 4

Revere, Paul, 6

San Francisco earthquake, 18–

seceded, 14, 16

settlement, 4

slaves, 16

space flight, 26–27

stock market, 24

territory, 17

World War I, 23

World War II, 25